Advance Praise

"In his memoir in verse, *At Sunset, Facing East*, Bill Jones records a life lived not just in years, but in voices, places, and dreams brave enough to defy time.... His collection maps uncharted routes between two rich horizons, pausing and marking his discoveries along the way. At long last, his 'secret ship' has arrived, sailing onto a shore where others can experience his powerful journey for themselves."

> —Katherine Cottle, Poet and Nonfiction Writer, Author of *My Father's Speech* and *I Remain Yours*

"In *At Sunset, Facing East*, Bill Jones nods to the absurdity and the sudden, surprising flashes of delight in our lives. Giant turtles disappear beneath the surface, a graveyard contains 'families like us,' a father's mysterious workplace turns out to contain governmental secrets, a two-year-old son teaches his poet-father about wisdom, and luckily for us, the father writes it all down."

> —Alicia Jo Rabins, Poet, Author of *Divinity School*, Winner of the 2015APR/Honickman First Book Prize

"Some poems aren't written. They're made direct. They skip the middle man. In *At Sunset, Facing East*, Bill Jones lets go of the self-consciousness of authorship and allows the poems to show themselves.... I could say plenty about the borderless reach of this book-length poetic memoir, but these self-illuminating poems say it better. What I can say is: Read Them."

> —Bruce A. Jacobs, Poet and Nonfiction Writer, Author of *Speaking Through My Skin* and *Race Manners*

"Bill Jones's *At Sunset, Facing East* is a collection of lyrical narrative poems that are as appealing to the ear as to the mind. Jones's stories transcend the quotidian to become allegories of the heart in love with family, friends, the natural beauty of the world, and life itself."

—Gary Blankenburg, Poet, Editor, Artist, Author of eight books of poetry, most recently *Above All Things*

"Bill Jones is an honest, engaging writer. His art doesn't strut before the reader but walks with purpose, opening doors then quietly stepping back to reveal the inner riches of experience.... If I was asked to recommend a book of poetry to get the educated general public interested in the art, I'd choose *At Sunset, Facing East*."

—Dan Cuddy, Poet, Editor of *Loch Raven Review*, Author of *Handprint on the Window*

At Sunset,
Facing East

At Sunset, Facing East

A Memoir in Poetry

Bill Jones

Apprentice House
Loyola University Maryland
Baltimore, Maryland

First Edition

Printed in the United States of America

Paperback ISBN: 978-1-62720-125-4
E-book ISBN: 978-1-62720-126-1

Design: Emily Jennings
Editorial Development: Luisa Beguiristain
Cover photo: Bill Jones
Author photo: Jane C. Jones

Published by Apprentice House

Apprentice House
Loyola University Maryland
4501 N. Charles Street
Baltimore, MD 21210
410.617.5265 • 410.617.2198 (fax)
www.ApprenticeHouse.com

info@ApprenticeHouse.com

For my family—
past, present, future

Contents

III

Traveling

IV

Dreams

I

1951-1969

"The Child is father of the Man..."

—William Wordsworth,
"My Heart Leaps Up"

Terrapin

A dark ghost-thing,
it swam out of the seagrass
beneath the surface of the shallow water—
a shadow, black,
large as a trashcan lid.

At first
as I stared down from the pier,
I thought my eyes were playing tricks,
perhaps a cloud had passed before the sun,
but when I realized what it was,
I raced onto the shore
and up the flagstone steps, shouting,
Someone come, someone come
to summon anyone to share
the voltage of that moment.

They stood,
Uncle Harold and my parents,
talking to themselves,
not interested in childish melodrama,
and when they came down,
not running as I wanted,
just half-speed walking,
despite my pulling at their hands,
my cries to hurry,
the turtle was, of course,
long gone, swimming
back into the deep,
that muddled darkness,

Memory.

Why I Have No Work
in the Museum of Modern Art

Red, sweet-scented Marilyn Monroe
lipstick was my medium of choice
as I created a canvas
of our bathroom walls,
their aqua semi-gloss enamel
a proper surface for a two-year-old's
slash and swirl masterpiece.
When my conscience called,
I altered the art
with pink bathroom towels
and a matching fuzzy rug.
To clean those up,
I turned to bleach
retrieved from the laundry room
and poured bountifully
on the bathroom floor.
That, too, proved a bad idea
when my wide-eyed mother
intervened.

A few months later,
I tried performance art,
practicing the aesthetics of power
and disappearance, turning
something into nothing,
flushing my sister's miniature
ceramic tea set down the toilet—
Spoon? Gone! Cup? Gone! Saucer? Gone!
—more than a dozen pieces
whizzed and whirled away
before my mother walked in again
and suggested I take up music.

Two Weeks, Age 4, 1955

After he parks the car,
my father crosses behind it
to the passenger side
to help my mother.

He walks with her slowly,
his arm around her
in her long, tweed coat,
leading her

to our front door
where my grandmother
moves me out of the way
to let them in.

Inside the house,
he guides my mother
back to their room
where I remember her

staying in the dark for days.
You'll have to be
the son for two,
my father speaks.

My brother Steven's gone—
he's lived two weeks.

Young William's Great Escape

(Frederick, MD, 1956)

At age five, a graduate of one
too many Lassie episodes,
I knew that running away
was serious business.
So I wrapped my necessities
in one of my father's handkerchiefs—
one pair of wears,
a change of socks,
and three silver dollars—
then hung the package on a stick
and hoisted it over my shoulder.

And I'd still be on the road today
if it hadn't been for John Mackley,
a skinny, tow-headed kid my age
who came out into his yard two blocks away
and started playing wiffle ball.
It wasn't that I'd ever been a friend of John's,
but the prospect of smacking that plastic ball
sure beat the hell out of a long night of walking,
bad sleeping under some azalea bush,
or huddling in a boxcar headed out of town.

So Mackleys' yard is where
my father found me,
helped me gather my traveling gear,
and hoisted me onto his back
to carry his hobo home.

On a Mission, Age 6

In the second grade
at St. John the Evangelist,
we'd sell subscriptions
to *The Catholic Review*
to earn a 5-inch white plastic statue
of Mary, the Mother of God,
who, if held over a hundred-watt
lightbulb for two minutes,
would glow in the dark,
a light lime green.

But in first grade,
our business had been even
more serious. To each of us,
Sister Iranese distributed cardboard
canisters with coin slots
in their enameled metal tops
and Jesus Himself on the side,
benign and beaming,
standing beneath palm trees
and azure skies, surrounded
by chubby infants—African,
Chinese, Indian, Eskimo—
each smiling and dressed
in native garb.

Dropping
our pennies through
the sacred slots each day,
our job was to fill our cans,
saving those pagan babies,
keeping them from Limbo,
their souls in our holy hands.

Morning Poem, Dividing Creek, 1957

We rose in the dark
in the split-shingled cottage,
my father, grandfather, and I.

One light over the dining table,
we drank fresh juice, ate cantaloupe,
without talking.

Out on the pier,
we loaded the boat by flashlight—
rods, tackle boxes, landing net,
basket, bucket, box of worms.

Through clouds, the sky first streaking pink,
ropes ringing masts in the point marina,
we backed the boat into the creek,
outboard rumbling, churning white.

Mallards scattered in our path,
veeing the water,
taking to the sky.

Isles of seaweed rode our wake,
green-leaved vines, alive
with nettles and darting shrimp.

Rounding the sandbar,
the locust post with its red lit lantern,
we three stood up behind the windshield,
my father at the wheel.

The sun in our faces,
wind chilling our arms,
we held our hats
and headed for the bay.

Full Twist

My grandfather Jones couldn't swim a lick.
The best I ever saw him do was float around
in one of those inflated truck tire innertubes,
pulling seaweed out of the Magothy.
But what he could do was teach diving.
He'd take the most knock-kneed,
teeth-chattering, skinny nine-year-old boy
and have him doing full twists and one-and-a-halfs
off the oak plank board
like Olympic guys in training.
Arc higher, he'd say, and Danny'd rise up higher.
Try an inward, he'd suggest, and Paul would do an inward.
No splash, he'd command, and we'd all harness our legs
and point our toes to cut in like a knife.
Now when I think about my grandfather,
I don't think of a man just
looking foolish in a big black rubber donut.
I think of a teacher's approving grin
as his students all took flight.

Diving Lesson

(Magothy River, MD, 1962)

When Danny went off
that board and landed
full-face in a nettle,
we all quit swimming
for the day.
His rise to the surface,
his hair still streaming
tentacles, blood-red and
white, the shriek he let out
as he cried for breath
and please
ease from the burn,
all made us think
that diving's not just
grace in air
but plunging into
darkness.

Catching Fireflies

(Frederick, MD, 1963)

We'd wade into the ragweed
fields at dusk and watch them rise,
black blur of wings and sudden flash.
Our backs against scrub oaks
and walnut trees, we'd stare
into the dying sky to spy
their silhouettes as they took flight.

John Rosapepe and I
had planned our fortune,
catching ten flies for a nickel
for the scientists at Detrick.
Missile tracking they said
they had in mind, some deep
space mission, and I imagined
yellow blinking of the dust
that smeared our fingers
as we took them from the nets.

At home another thought took life
as the flies went into the freezer
with the ones from nights before.
As we'd dump our catch
into the icy mason jars,
the ones already frozen
would twitch and come alive,
arise from sleep as though
nothing had ever happened.
One August night we stood
transfixed as fly after fly
crawled from the jars
and filled my mother's kitchen.

So what were we to think?
Was it the flashing that transformed
those bugs into laboratory gold,
or was it frozen death not death
that drew the men of science?
Maybe both. Consider:

Somewhere beyond the stars
a secret ship is sailing,
its crew on ice,
not quite ready to glow.
Just as it hits the light
of yet one more horizon,
it's in a net.
Two wondering boys run off,
their cosmic pennies jingling.

Chain, Lake Goshen, VA, 1963

Dive! the head guard shouted,
and we dove, thirty pairs of legs
scissoring the air
as we pulled ourselves
into the green of Goshen,
hoping to hit rock bottom.
What we didn't hope was
to touch the missing boy—
his hands, his hair, his legs,
disappeared at buddy check,
now settled somewhere
as this chain of divers,
eleven and twelve years old,
worked its way,
one body length at a time,
some eight feet down,
in search of flesh turned marble cool,
in search of a boy turned blue.

Debridement

The process of removing damaged flesh from a wound,
debridement promotes healing and minimizes scarring.

In the early 60s
in the warfare labs at Detrick,
an autoclave boiled over,
scalding my father's legs
from a few inches above the knees
to the place his shoes protected.
There were no burn units
in hospitals then, so my father,
a medic in France in World War II,
chose to come home
to care for himself
on the couch in our living room.
With white sheets
covering the cushions,
he'd sit, his legs wrapped
in gauze and yellow medication
until it came time
to change the bandages.
And that's where I came in,
unwrapping as he instructed,
slowly, delicately,
handling the relics
of his calves and shins
and then, with surgical scissors
and a scalpel, removing
what had died, taking it
to the very edge
of what was living.

What I remember most
was the look on my father's face
as I, at ten years old,
would clip, then lightly scrape.
He'd bite his lip and
occasionally close his eyes.
Go on! he'd say. *Go on!*
as I did my best not
to hurt this man who would not
cry out, not once.
And then, the ointment re-applied,
we'd wrap, slowly, carefully,
the bandages,
mummying his legs,
relieved to have this over
until it was time for the two of us
to change again.

What I Know About Anthrax

As a child, all I knew was
that my father worked with monkeys,
chimpanzees mostly,
in a lab at Fort Detrick, Maryland.
Once in a while he would describe
the chimp he liked the most
or one that had escaped that day.

At the time, none of us,
children of researchers at Detrick,
knew what our fathers did.
None of us knew that
our mothers had signed
an agreement that they'd never see
our fathers' bodies again
if something went wrong in the labs.

From the 1950s until 1969,
when President Richard Nixon announced
a shutdown of the United States'
biological warfare program,
Fort Detrick was one of the world's largest
producers of anthrax.

The biological warfare program
conducted studies on human volunteers,
"white coats," who were conscientious
objectors, often Seventh-day Adventists.
Their alternative to Detrick was serving
as medics in Vietnam.

During World War II,
my father was a medic in France.
Most of the Detrick researchers I knew
were veterans with combat experience
in German-occupied Europe.
They believed our nation would
only survive with the scientific
upper hand. They were the fathers
of my friends.

My father worked three jobs
to support my mother and our family.
He cashiered at a People's drugstore,
sold Christmas cards door to door,
and worked in the labs at Detrick.
He regularly came home sore-armed
from the inoculations that were requirements
of his employment.

Two men died in the Detrick anthrax lab,
one a scientist who'd made procedural mistakes,
the other an electrician who'd entered the lab,
against regulations, after having dental surgery.
My father was handed test tubes containing
the ashes of the one man's body
to certify that his anthrax
was no longer alive.

My strongest memory of my father
from this period
is seeing him on his knees
late at night by the bed
where my mother was sleeping.
His head was down,
and he didn't see me watching
as he prayed.

Years after the anthrax lab was closed,
my father worked at Detrick
in a commercial site,
one of the world's largest production labs
for interferon,
a cancer-fighting agent.

The week of my father's funeral,
my mother gave me a letter
from the federal government
that stated that a volunteer
follow-up study had found
that the men who'd been repeatedly
inoculated at Detrick
had suffered no long-term,
life-threatening effects.

After the warfare center closed,
there was a building at Fort Detrick,
a tower of six or seven stories,
which was sealed up,
windows bricked,
for over forty years.
That building now has disappeared.
A new "biodefense" laboratory,
built in 2008,
has taken its place.

That's what I know
about anthrax.
You make a poem from it
if you can.

Sanctuary

I remember the smell and touch
of altar wax, the hot flash,
then soothing peeling off,
and I still see the glinting
monstrance with the two-inch host
bound in gilt sunrays.
Incense still fills my senses
as do ringing bells
at the host's greatest height—
holy, holy, holy.
I hear my father thump his chest,
my grandmother's clicking beads,
her whistling, whispered prayers.
The purple Lenten vestments
yet caress my face
as I try to burrow
back into that sacred time
when God still came to Earth
for all His simple children.

II

1970-2015

"Instructions for living a life:
Pay attention.
Be astonished.
Tell about it."

—Mary Oliver,
"Sometimes"

College Boy

(Olean, New York, 1970)

October nights,
I'd close the pool
and head back to the dorms.
Through scarlet maples
one block off State,
cones of light spilled
from lampposts onto lawns.
And more light called
from clapboard houses,
sheer-draped rectangles
giving glimpses of the world—
supper served,
Bless us, O Lord,
baked chicken,
parsley garnish.
And I'd drive by
in cricket darkness,
windows down
in first fall air,
wanting hard
to pull in somewhere,
bound up steps
and through the door.
I'm home, Mom.
What's for dinner?
and these thy gifts,
pass the potatoes,
please.

Dawn, A Monday Morning

(Lancaster, PA, 1971)

It's dawn,
a Monday morning,
and I'm driving the Fairlane
through Lancaster cornfields,
all shocks and husks,
their scent as dark as coffee.
I'm reigned in, doing twenty-five,
behind an Amish carriage,
while the driver,
straw hat and sloping shoulders,
holds back a sorrel
who keeps veering off the road.
I'm moving now
on automatic pilot,
thinking of Jane's eyes,
her fingers on my face,
her lips,
and two more months
wishing the weeks away,
our lives reduced
to letters and long distance
from one three-day visit
to the next.

Physics for Poets

(St. Bonaventure University, Spring 1972)

Maybe the science department
was having mercy on us,
trying to help us graduate,
or it was padding its enrollments,
saving an assistant professor or two,
but either way we'd gather each week
for two ninety-minute sessions,
sixty long-haired art and English
majors, armed with spiral notebooks
and Flair pens, to be enlightened
about the wonders of science
and its aesthetic applications.
In the only lecture I clearly remember,
I was staring out the windows at the Enchanted
Mountains across the Allegheny,
my mind filled with William Blake
and the potential for speaking to angels.
Behind the podium, Professor Neeson,
all crewcut, hornrims, and pocket protector,
had launched into matters of motion and time,
the realms of Albert Einstein.
Humans who traveled in rockets, he claimed,
returned to Earth younger than their buddies.
William Blake would have loved that notion,
but then, at twenty, I could only understand
the relative truth that in that course
called Physics for Poets,
we students were happy
just going through the motions,
putting in the time,
our teachers rapidly aging
as we stayed young
in space.

Learning to Walk, Baltimore, 1973

A few months after I've moved into the city,
I'm driving the Datsun west
through the no man's land of Franklin
when I turn left across
what I think is a parking lane
and am smacked by a Yellow Cab.
By the time the crunching's done,
I'm leaning right at a forty-five
degree angle, hanging by my seatbelt.
The cabby, a black man,
maybe twenty-two,
is fine.
His heavy Dodge, a bloated shark,
is barely scratched.

As we're sitting at curbside, waiting
for what I hope will be a cop,
a white deVille pulls up,
lit coach lanterns on its sides,
a diamond-shaped window in its landau roof.
I know this car is one of four, all white,
that cruise downtown,
heart, spade, and club cars
patrolling other regions.

When a tinted window glides down,
I'm face to face with another black man
in his twenties,
slick, white-suited,
with two smooth women in satin red,
who smile at me, not speaking.
You OK? the diamond man calls
to the shook-up cabby, who says he is

before the Cadillac drives off,
and all at once, the sidewalk's filled
with dancing, laughing project kids,
elementary boys and girls,
who sing with glee,
Honky's gonna get it now!

Six weeks later in District Court,
I luck out
with Probation Before Judgment,
then borrow court costs and bus fare
because my car's in the shop
and all I've got's a check.
On the way home, at Charles and 25th,
my bus sideswipes some tan sedan
and is filled with victims screaming,
My neck! My back! My ankle!
I hit the emergency door
and walk those last blocks home.

Before Flight

(Forest Park, Baltimore, 1974)

My grandmother and grandfather wait
on the steps to their bedrooms
as a young man's hand reaches
through the just-broken glass beside their front door
when he thinks they're not at home.

In that house, where they are the last
white people on their street,
the fog lifts one January morning
and someone's posted
a For Sale sign on their lawn.

My second cousin,
who lives six blocks away,
calls home routinely from work
to see if anyone will answer
in his empty house.

One morning someone does.
One 9-1-1 call
and two bullet holes in the attic later,
his home becomes a feature
on the 6 and 11 news.

Going Back to Bill's

Some things die hard they say.
Some things die very hard.

In this yard, we hid as children,
lying still beneath just-raked piles,
oak leaves touching our faces
like brittle widow's hands.

The family gathered in this house,
a white clapboard on Garrison,
six full bedrooms, a trellised porch,
the luscious scent of lilac.

Now we go back twice a month
to check on things, to sweep up plaster,
and take out what remains—an old TV,
a stack of letters, the last of my cousin's clothes.

Each time there is a new surprise—
pigeons in the attic
through a fresh hole in the roof.
A gray rat, stone dead,

on the walk back to the alley.
A door bashed in,
put to rest by nailing shut
with a handful of sixteens.

Then things step up.
Under the leaves, a monkey carcass,
shaved, cut up, inside a burlap sack.
In the garage, an old mattress,

broken pints, the calling cards of winos.
One Saturday, an abandoned car,
an '86 Olds, stripped, up on blocks,
a shell of pulled out wires.

And finally, a body,
a woman in her thirties,
stabbed six times,
wrapped in a blanket.

A dark pool and white chalk marks
left to be washed away.
Use hot water and bleach,
the detective recommends.

The family gathered in this house.
In this yard we hid as children.
Some things die very hard.

To Sean, 1981

For weeks before you came, Sean,
I'd go at night into your room,
sit quietly in the cherry rocker,
and wonder about you.

Then you were born,
slick wet in the doctor's hands,
pink and squawling,
with an old man's wrinkles
and clear, dark eyes.
I held you fast, took you to Mom;
we cried and laughed
together.

Those first few weeks,
close to my chest, you'd rest asleep,
your whole hand gripping my one finger,
your breathing quiet, your eyes soft shut,
your feet in the palm of my hand.
I'd tuck them inside your cotton gown
to keep you warm.

Mornings we'd wake and go downstairs.
Singing songs, we'd open curtains,
look for birds and count the leaves.
Sometimes we'd walk the steps together;
I'd talk of forests, mountain snow.
I told you tales about the ocean,
promised nights asleep in pines.

And now you wake me with your singing;
you squeal and clamber up the steps.
You empty closets, point out airplanes,
patter-slap across the floor.
We play in bathtubs, climb on couches;
I stack up blocks; you knock them down.
We sit together, getting shoes on;
you hold the socks; I take my time.

And still at night,
while you are sleeping,
I like to come into your room.
I stand and watch your quiet breathing.
I stand and wonder—
you are my son.

Lesson: Looking at the Moon

At two years old,
my son Sean was fascinated
with the moon.
He'd spot it in the ink-dark sky
or pale and fading in morning light.
Touch it, Dad, he'd say,
then stretch both hands, fingers wide,
up into the stars.
Touch it, he'd repeat,
standing on tiptoes,
then looking up to me,
his gray eyes round and shining.

And so I'd stretch my hands
above him, reaching,
pretending to touch,
trying hard to forego truth
to share his vision,
bright as any moon.

Thought, While Walking with My Two-Year-Old Daughter

In my grandmother's first memory of her father,
he walked with her too fast, her hand in his,
so she was half-lifted from her feet,
a child with auburn, curly hair,
looking up in wonder
at a man with giant strides.

Right off the boat from County Kilkenny,
he had taken a wife in Philadelphia,
then come to Baltimore to drive a coach
and later serve up cold ones
in his bar on Stockton street.
He died when my grandmother was ten.

Some eighty years later,
she sat with me in a Frederick nursing home,
her legs still, beneath an afghan,
her hands, with knuckles large as walnuts,
folding and re-folding a paper napkin
on her day-chair tray.

She spoke of this man
in her memory
as though he were some distant god,
a Celtic king come down to Earth
for too short a time
to be her father.

Nightsong, 3:39 A.M.

A cry bursts white
into my sleep
as 3-year-old Sara's footsteps
pummel the carpet
into our room.
A dream, Daddy,
a dream! she calls,
and I flip off the radio
that's been playing in the dark,
Martha Reeves' *nowhere to run*
still sounding in my head.

I know they're back,
the flying monkeys,
her nightly haunters
since her visit with the Wizard
three weeks ago.
So I pick her up
and walk the hall
back to her room,
soothing her to rest again.
The Vandellas' tune yet haunting me,
I find myself burying my face
in her sweet blonde hair.

Yes, I find myself
with a 3-year-old, thinking,
keep running, baby,
keep running,
'cause someday it won't be
the dreams you'll fear
but the lack of dreams,

and there won't be arms
to lift you up
to hold you tight
while phantom women wail.
No emerald slippers, honey,
nowhere to hide.

Families, North Carolina, 1988

They won't hurt you; come on in, says Jane,
so the three of us step through the barbed wire gate.
Over the ridge from Tennessee we've strayed,
misread a map, and ended in this place.
Sean's seven, Sara's only three.
She rides my shoulders, worn out from the heat.
Drawn to the shade beneath the hemlock trees,
we took this path to see where it might lead.
The plot is small, the markers simply made—
names, dates of death, carved in sandy stone.
They're families like us; I'm not afraid,
Jane tells the kids and me. In quiet tones,
she reads the names of *James* and *Henry Orr,*
then clears the weeds from *Mary Jenkins, 1904.*

"Plane Crashes in Towson, Killing Pilot"

—*The Baltimore Sun, November 12, 1988*

How was I to know
as I drove south on York Road
that all those unfocused moments
of death I had witnessed
were hurtling toward this one spiral
from the sky?
Hands on the wheel in traffic,
I was living them again—
the film clip kick
of John Kennedy's head rocking
into Jackie's arms,
the Sunday surrealism
in the Dallas police station
as fat Jack Ruby in his slouched hat
stepped up to the handcuffed Oswald
and blasted him,
the nightly numbing riots
in Watts, Newark, Baltimore,
storefronts on fire,
shotguns blazing,
flames and bullets becoming
life enroute to Vietnam,
where men now given
one black marble wall
went down to death each day
for ABC.
I just looked up
to see him falling,
spinning oh so slowly
like those balsa gliders we all had,
then arcing into air show heaven

till he leveled off at cloud line.
Then he was gone,
gone,
become a dark smoke column
shooting into blue,
far above this world we live in
where men sprint screaming
for their short, sweet lives,
and click off death before a game show,
and run for answers when it's falling
from the sky.

Mother Country, 2 A.M.

Six weeks before Nathan's birth,
I'm awake, Jane against me,
warm, belly taut
as a medicine ball
but moving, moving,
turning the Sealy
into a water bed.
Jane sleeps in quiet,
unaware of that
stretching knee or fist
touching me
through her body wall,
demanding to be born.

She's in that country
where no man's ever been,
where women drift
from husbands, lovers,
a land of tremors
and ocean sounds,
silent swimmers,
water warm as blood.

It's that world
she's peering into
that final time,
her eyes focused
through rhythmic breathing,
when Nathan's born
on one last wave,
crashing into
the father land.

Walking with Nathan, 1992

September evenings
we walk the loop road
that makes up the neighborhood—
Nathan two, me forty.
Step and stop, step and stop,
he leads me by the hand.
We hunt for toads or leopard frogs
hiding under hosta,
or toss rocks down the storm drain,
just to hear the plop.
As nighthawks glide by overhead
into the coming darkness,
I'm reminded of Tiresias,
the ancient Greek,
who saw the Truth
but could not see the sky.
Helpless, blind,
he trailed a boy
who shared his living vision.
So Nathan guides me into sunset
as crickets start their chant.
This wise, young son
travels in circles,
showing his father the way.

House Sounds, 1 A.M.

There is no quiet in our darkened house—
the plaster creaks with sixty years of weight,
the furnace fills its hissing lungs with gas,
exhales warm wind through clinking metal grates.
The refrigerator launches itself in sound,
its compressor whistling like a day-old bird,
the hamster turns its plastic wheel around
as Sara mutters restless, dreaming words.
The boys are rolling in their squeaking beds.
Beside me, Jane is sighing in her sleep.
I scribble thoughts that scramble from my head,
flip off the light with hope that they will keep.
Outside, the late night cars go gliding home
into imperfect silence of their own.

Outside the Kindergarten Classroom

Inside, another set of parents are learning
about their child, assignment by assignment,
skill by skill. Outside, I'm looking
for my son's name on charts of favorite colors
and scents he smelled on Friday.
I find his painting of a fall day—
a tree with twenty apples,
in the air a cardinal, a scarlet V in the sky,
the first blush of a pink-blue sunset.
Here, on this folding metal chair,
I see the two sides of this boy
we all call Nathan—the five-year-old
student who spends each afternoon
in this first of many classrooms
and the boy who blooms with laughter
when he sprints from the schoolhouse door.

One Patron, One Explorer

The raptors and T. rex
are raising their nasty heads,
and I think Nate may be over his,
a fourth grader trying to read Crichton.
He claims he's mastered decoding skills
and context clues, but they don't help him
with "rapacious" in this *Jurassic Park*
he's found in his brother's closet.
Try "vicious and starving," I suggest,
and he goes quiet for a while.
What's "patron"? he follows up,
and I propose "customer"
until he demands
that I hear the sentence.
How about "supporter,"
I offer, *or "provider of money,"*
as in "providing patronage"?
Oh, you mean like Isabella
and Columbus, Nathan clarifies,
and I say, *Yes, that's what I mean*
exactly.

In the Cathedral of Cezanne

(Philadelphia Museum of Art, 1996)

Trapped in a marble hall in this mass of pilgrims,
Sara and I snake our way toward the Cezanne exhibit
amid hundreds of tour guide headsets
that chirp like yellowjackets
caught in paper cups.
Can you hear, Sal? Can you hear?
the lady behind me asks her husband,
who can't quite master the controls.
Art patrons line up, dressed to kill,
sipping fine wine from plastic glasses.
A guy in a tuxedo folds his music
and closes the baby grand. It's 9 p.m.

Inside the gallery,
security guards in stiff white shirts
shrug their shoulders to keep awake.
A silver-haired man in a sportcoat and ascot
perches before each painting on his cane,
the handle folding to create a seat,
his wife caught on the crook of his arm.
A twenty-year-old guides his brother in a wheelchair,
leaning so close over him that it looks as though
he'll kiss the trembling face.
And in room after room, ladies in their summer
silks stand transfixed by the splendor
of the Frenchman's art—
Mont Sainte-Victoire looming beyond the pines;
L'Estaque, a golden-roofed village by the sea;
a bend in the road near a villa in Marseilles;
and most of all, the glades of bathing women,
posed in portraits lush enough to taste.
Again and again, Cezanne returns to them,
hushing the rooms to silence.

Outside, after the show, the sky is warm;
the stars and moon glide overhead in brilliance;
in the distance, August thunder rumbles;
from the river, crickets call,
Cezanne.

Smitty's Auto & Truck

Nate and I've got the end-of-the-weekend
blues, me with piles of paperwork
and Nate with a ton of sixth grade math,
so we've taken a field trip to Anne Arundel County,
home of Smitty's Auto & Truck,
"Recyclers of Quality Used Auto Parts,"
to pick up a little something for Sean's Honda.

Four miles off Ritchie Highway lies
Smitty's, which some consider Mecca,
a full ten acres of car and truck carcasses
with an occasional golf cart
wedged into old white oaks and mud,
all hidden behind an eight-foot
aluminum fence.

We're sitting on the verandah
of the cinderblock establishment
that smells mostly of dust and axle grease
after we've placed our order inside
and Smitty's sent his man off roaring
into the wilderness in a '73 Dodge
with no muffler or backseat.

There's silence in the distance
as the guy stops to wrench our part from vehicle 1742,
an Accord whose family sold its body into auto afterlife.
Meanwhile, Nate and I relax on a rusty glider
in the late September sun, speculating
about how that Mr. Softee truck landed on its side
without its windshield cracking

and when those two feral cats
with murder in their eyes
will commence to fighting,
or where old Smitty got those six life-size
plastic geese in full Harley regalia
standing guard over a meadow
of aluminum spinning daisies.

Some ten minutes later, a quarter-mile away,
the old Dodge thunders to life
and bucks its way out of the muck
with Smitty's man grinning and our Japanese
jack handle bungee-corded to his hood.
You can always salvage something
on a Sunday afternoon.

The Ordinary

(Hidden Valley, PA, 1996)

"The ordinary can be like medicine."
        —Sherman Alexie

At night it's falling asleep
to Sara and Kaitlin's giggles
and the sounds of Sean and John,
both taller now than I am,
playing five-card in the living room.
The next day it's fishing with Nathan,
a three-pound largemouth flopping
off his hook and splattering us,
laughing, with mud.
Each afternoon there's swimming,
length by length in the clear, cool pool,
beneath late August sky.
At two a.m. it's moonlight
gazing through the window
as Jane turns in her sleep
and I brush her hair back
from that face I've loved
for nearly thirty years.

To Sara, 1999

Nearly sixteen years ago,
you made your way into this world,
calm and quiet, with none
of the fuss or emergency
of Sean and Nate.
Mom didn't break a sweat.
When you started crawling,
you strutted, hands gaiting out
like a Tennessee Walker's,
your head held high, eyes gleaming.
You swam at three, floating
to the pool's surface in Fontana
and paddling away.
Tonight, fifteen, you're boarding
a plane to Ireland by yourself
on your first flight, seven hours
in the dark across the Atlantic
to land in Shannon at dawn.
Backpack in place,
you walk the long corridor
beyond where Mom and I can go.
We stand there, grinning,
watching and waving,
as you pass through security
and emerge on the other side.

More Testimony

(Baltimore, September 11, 2001)

That morning as I left writing class,
Matt came in to tell me
that a plane had flown into the World
Trade Center, and by the time
I got downstairs, the second plane
had hit, and then it all came down,
the third plane at the Pentagon,
the fourth missing, then down
in Pennsylvania.

At school, all TVs were tuned
to death. Again and again,
that plane melted like butter
into that tower's side,
then people leapt onto the concrete
that many of us had walked.
We had safe rooms for those who didn't
want to watch, and counselors' rooms,
and rooms for phone calls
where students could check
on ones they loved
with teachers standing by to comfort.
At eleven, stationed at the back
school entrance, I met parents,
directing them to the office
to take their children home.

That afternoon, Sara, Nate, and I
sat in the basement talking, watching more,
then waiting for Jane to arrive
from the office to plan our calls
to Sean in Delaware, and to our parents
and sisters and brothers, and to Shannon
in Manhattan, and to Steve and Ray to check
on their daughters at NYU.

Around seven, I went to Meadowbrook
to swim outdoors in the fifty meter pool,
back and forth, back and forth,
beneath a sky now blue and peach,
a sky now empty in Baltimore,
save that one plane melting
into that tower, again and again,
until it grew too dark, and the guard said
it was time for me to go.

Two Brothers, Ages 45 and 50, Appear to Be Fishing on Fenwick State Park Beach

(Delaware, 2002)

The wind from the shore is eerily warm,
the breeze from the surf is cool.
It looks like Tom and I
know what we're doing.

We lug the tackle box,
two nine-foot rods,
two folding chairs,
and a bucket of mullet
down the beach for the afternoon,
past the last van and surf truck,
staking our claim, baiting up,
and casting our hopes into the water.
Tom's ready for a sand shark.
I'm waiting on the blues.

Two hours later, after catching
nothing, Tom has lost his third rig,
and I'm just pitching past the breakers
and waiting for the lures to wash ashore.
By the end, we're whipping
three ounce sinkers out
to see how far they'll go.
As late afternoon drifts
into evening, the wind picks up
and fills the tackle box with sand.

Back at the house
some twelve blocks south,
six kids,
two wives,
one sister and her husband,
two grandparents,
and assorted others
fuss over what's for supper
and where those two
old brothers can be.

It looks like Tom and I
know what we're doing.
The wind from the shore is eerily warm,
the breeze from the surf is cool.

Three Men in the Hospital, Shaving

In the silver-blue scent
of electricity,
they lift their chins
when I ask, their faces dry
as are their mouths, their lips,
their tongues. IVs don't do
much to ward off thirst.
These men, their eyes,
their voices are tired.
Within days they will be
tired no longer. They say
they feel better,
thanking me—
my grandfather, 1976,
my father, 2003.

What This Photograph Won't Tell You

This photograph is just
the face of a man,
eighty-five years old,
gleaming, grinning,
like a boy
maybe six,
his eyes crinkled,
hair swept to the side,
in a one-inch square
atop his obituary.

What this photograph won't tell you
is that there'd been no time to waste
getting to the pond in Middletown
and setting up at the end
where we knew they'd be biting
on the wooly hawgs
if we had some patience
and rigged them right.

And if you saw it all,
uncropped, you'd know
that August night was cool,
near perfect, the breezes light,
the sky gone pink from blue,
overhead the flights of Canadians
heading south, the moon rising
full over Braddock Mountain
where his cabin waited,
and his face was bright because
on the end of his line
was one fine largemouth,
Mike Croghan's last fish,
before the darkness dropped
and he headed, finally, home.

Talking with Joe, 2008

Please don't stop talking, he said.
I might not always be able to answer,
but your talking means a lot to me.

And I thought about this cousin,
more like a brother, and how we'd been together
since our early sandbox days,

and of our years making films, writing songs,
painting each other's houses, laughing like madmen
while punning on the phone.

Those last few months, he was tired
but not defeated. He had friends to see and a new bass
calling for a few more runs.

And, of course, he had a funeral to plan—
paintings he wanted hung by his coffin,
musicians to invite, a play list to request—

"Desperado,"
"Please Don't Bury Me,"
"I'll Fly Away."

And he told me how he should be dressed—
sunglasses on, the cobalt blue shirt
with the Cancer Sucks button in place.

With all that ready,
I talked as he sat, usually smoking,
skeleton-thin, day after day,

on his couch turned into a bed,
his eyes closed,
his head cocked to the side

as though he were listening
to something I was not yet
ready to hear.

Even When You Think It's Winter

(in the voice of Joe Flaherty, 1952-2008)

In the misty distance
lies the town I've left,
walking last steps along
a stream you've glimpsed
but never followed.
In it, small rapids rattle
the rocks. The water's cold
and deeper than it seems.
But here it's quiet and calm,
late spring warm,
even when you think it's winter.
Trees without leaves are mirrored
clearly in the silver pool.
When I look in, I see
what's there is beautiful.
In it, I see myself and
you.

A Teacher's Thoughts at Graduation

Each year, the orders
would come in to the boatyard
on Dividing Creek,
the scaffolds would come out of storage,
and the oak skeletons would appear
for weeks of transformation—
oyster boats, maybe, pleasure cruisers,
long-sterned fishing vessels,
all marked by that high-prowed bow,
parting water clear as ice
on that first trip up the Magothy.

And that same trip would be their last
away from the boatyard,
away from the craftsmen with razor chisels,
piled blond curls of oak,
sheer scent rising
from buckets of shellac.

Three Times Seeing Quentin

The first time I saw Quentin, 1977,
his greeting was simple, self-assured:
I'm going to break your jaw.
This from a student who'd come to me for help,
a black kid in a trench coat,
fifteen years old,
six-four, two-twenty,
placed in this school by the courts
and scheduled with me
three times a week for tutoring.
Each time he'd come into the room,
he'd say the line about my jaw.
Have a seat, Quentin, I'd answer,
we've got work to do.
He finished the semester
and was gone.

November 16, 1984, 11 p.m.,
the lower parking lot of Sinai Hospital.
Eighteen minutes before the birth
of my daughter, Sara, I was on my way
to the Labor and Delivery entrance,
up three substantial hills and sets of steps
with my wife, Jane, a woman so stubborn
that she refused to be dropped off.
I want to walk, she said. *No wheelchair routine
this time; it'll keep the labor going.*
So we walked, her arm around my shoulder,
the two of us stopping every few seconds
for her to breathe, breathe, breathe, then blow.
You get the picture. Well, so did Quentin.
As we reached the second level,
he emerged from the pines along the stairway,
staggering a little.

Hey, Quentin, how you doing?
This from me, sizing up the chances.
His eyes cold and cloudy as a winter night,
Quentin passed us by.

The last time I saw Quentin, 1992.
I was in the basement with Nate,
my third child, two years old.
Quentin was on TV, downtown in a park,
a microphone in his face,
traffic streaming in the background,
little boys clowning to get on camera.
As always, there was the trench coat.
The reporter, all blonde and business suit,
riddled him with questions.
As poised as a college professor,
Quentin answered her.
Quentin, Homeless, Mentally Ill—
This from the caption beneath his face.

After 40 Years of Teaching English, I Retire

But often, in the din of strife,
There rises an unspeakable desire
After the knowledge of our buried life...
—Matthew Arnold, "The Buried Life"

After forty years of teaching English,
I've decided to free my mind
in old and new directions,
no longer worried about schedules and assignments
and the best ways to present truth and beauty,
with no more hours and hours of editing and grading
and annotating everything I read.

I will miss the inspiration that flashed every day
in every classroom in student after student
and in myself. I will miss the sense of doing something
noble, of passing on the heritage of learning
handed down to me by teachers who understood
truth and beauty and youth,
who cared more about teaching than anything.

But now, I plan to practice what I've taught—
to unbury myself in the wake of Matthew Arnold,
to search for Walden in this place where I live,
to remain a child like Wordsworth,
unfettered by Frost's promises to keep.

At Sunset, Facing East

(Pompano Beach, Florida, October 2014)

At sunset, facing east,
retired, I'm on the beach alone,
watching the changing
sky and water
until the light is gone.

I've spent almost fifty years
driving myself
full throttle west,
thinking I had to get somewhere
before I'd stop for rest.

As azure fades to indigo
and pinks become deep reds,
I give thanks for both horizons
and for the darkness rich with stars
in this place all roads have led.

My Mother, Eighty-Nine

Eighty-nine years old and living
in the nursing home where
her own mother died at ninety-three,
my mother spends her days in a wheelchair
where she's sat for the last few years.
Though she's with others every day,
hymn-singing, doing arts and crafts,
and playing games, her mind
has plenty of time to wonder.

Did you know that my parents are both alive?
she asked during a recent weekly visit.
She said they came to see her, sometimes
together, once in a rickety boat that
was ready to sink by the nurse's station.
She saw her father in a room once,
playing with a group of toddlers.
He seemed so happy, she said. *I didn't
realize that he loved children so much.*

She has conversations
with great-grandchildren
framed in photographs on the wall.
Sometimes she sings to them.
She speaks frequently of how my father,
whom she calls "my husband,"
never using his name,
once helped the biblical Noah,
catching fish for the starving animals in the ark.

So I shouldn't have been surprised
when at the end of our last visit
after a nice talk, mostly about her memories,
she asked me who I was.

Sixty-Three

It takes a long time to become young.
—Pablo Picasso

Opening blinds to welcome morning light,
listening for the silver sounds of birds,
searching for a crescent moon at night,
discovering the jumbled joy of words,
watching fan blades quickly changing speeds,
eating berries till they're nearly gone,
climbing steps on both our hands and knees,
learning *open*, *shut*, and *off* and *on*,
paging through bright books of trucks and zoos,
mimicking and making crazy faces,
trying on those brand-new, velcroed shoes,
seeking out the best of hiding places—
after sixty-three years, I'm becoming young
with my grandson, Garrett, who's just one.

With Hands and Heartbeats

(November 13, 2015)

Sean's hands are huge, quick, sure
as he wraps Molly, his day-old daughter,
in a cotton hospital blanket.

He's changed her diaper
and covered her hair that's as dark as his
with a pastel infant's cap.

When he lifts her to his shoulder,
he pats her softly on the back, a move
Jane and I used when he was one day old.

If you pat her in a rhythm like a heartbeat,
he says, *she goes right to sleep.*
We smile, we know; we did the same for him,

and may Molly someday do the same for hers
with hands and heartbeats
in that time when love begins.

III

Traveling

"Travel far enough, you meet yourself."

—David Mitchell,
Cloud Atlas

Taking in the Sights

(Florida Keys, 1973)

This girl we met on Big Pine Key
gave us the tour—
a lagoon near her family's place
where a pair of dolphins, slick and gray,
would swim in to play with us
then head out to open water;
the abandoned highway bridge
where two men lived
diving for lobster by day,
celebrating each night
in their bright orange tent
beneath a scarlet sky;
a second lagoon where fish-cleaners
dumped their heads, guts, and skeletons,
soon to be targeted by forty or fifty fins
roiling the water, tarpon gliding in to feast;
Key deer at streams beneath the pines,
fully antlered, quiet as ghosts,
smaller than nine-year-old boys;
and finally, a clearing in the woods,
palm trees and cinder block houses
shredded by machine gun fire
as men emptied themselves out
before invading history
at the Bay of Pigs.

Natural Wonders

(Natural Bridge, VA, 1973)

I knew Michael was steamed when we walked
away from the ticket booth six dollars poorer.
They have no right to charge for this,
he said. *Natural wonders belong to us.*
So I shouldn't have been surprised when
we followed the gravel trail up the river,
past the arch with George Washington's initials,
another hundred yards to the wishing pool
formed by a ledge in the stream bed.
With the crowd thinned out and all that silver
flashing up, Michael couldn't contain himself.
They're quarters! he yelped as he stripped off
his shirt and shoes and jumped in to retrieve
his admission. And I shouldn't have been
surprised when he came up gasping,
wild-eyed, shocked by the cold and the current
and the twelve feet of water, and I knew
I had to help him, not only pulling him out
so he wouldn't drown, but plunging in myself
to save his honor, then walking out
ten minutes later with him, grinning,
tourists parting in our path
as we sloshed our way back to the car, jingling,
two dollars' worth of nickels in our pockets.

The Day the South Won the War

(Mountain Home, AR, 1973)

We drove all day out of Memphis
across the Mississippi
and up to Mountain Home
because that name had Southern charm
and the map said it had a lake.
Michael wanted the Ozarks,
and I wanted a swim.

We pulled in late that afternoon
and followed some kids to a swimming hole
where the water was cold and emerald clear
and the fish flashed up like silver.
From there we headed into Bull Shoals Park
above the dam to watch the sun
bed down in pink and purple,
the mountains misty as a dream.

Let's stay here, Michael said, and so we did,
flopping our bags out on the ground
to talk and sleep the sleep of Jesus
under stars.

At dawn, two pairs of sparkling black
trooper shoes nudged us awake,
opening our eyes with words of welcome—
*You boys know that camping here's
against the law? Clear out in five minutes
or we're locking y'all up.*

Seeing these fellows were in no mood
for compromise, we yes-sirred
our way back to the car,
packed our stuff in double-time,
and high-tailed our scrawny Northern
butts across the line to Missouri
to find ourselves some breakfast.

Third World

(Mexico, 1973)

Along the blazing road to Monterrey,
in the desert south of Brownsville,
children sold the pelts of chipmunks for pesetas.
That night, in a bar with ice-blue lights, a girl,
maybe seventeen, urged me to go upstairs with her
so she could pay her bills.

The next morning, as I watched,
a vendor carved meat from a goat's skull,
and a streetsweeper without legs
walked by on his hands
dragging a broom behind him
with his teeth.

Five days later, in Guanajuato,
city of silver, a two-year-old
with eyes as dark as the coffee
I was drinking, held out her hand
to me for coins, her mother
supervising from the shadows.

That's where I found myself
over forty years ago, facing truths
that made me who I am, not
in the waking world or the dreaming world,
but in a third world,
that land where the two collide.

Buen Apetito

(Guanajuato, Mexico, 1973)

Loco! Loco! they all shouted
as they rambled through the streets,
slapping Michael on the back,
crowning him with laughter,
their whacked-out gringo hero.

Yeah, those local boys went crazy
as he slugged down the last
of their mezcal, worm and all,
kissing his fingertips
and smacking his lips
to proclaim his zest
for eating pickled insects.

*What they don't know won't
hurt them,* he whispered to me
as minutes passed
and they went on serenading.
Then out from his cheek,
where he kept his chaw,
he plucked what looked
like a beetle grub
and flung it in the bushes.

Local Custom

(Mexico, 1973)

On the twisting snake of highway
rising west of Mexico City, we see
the people walking with their buckets.
Old men, hobbling like their burros,
clutching canes; chicos y chiquitas
on holiday, heading up the gravel shoulder,
laughing like mountain sparrows;
young couples holding hands and smiling—
all carry their buckets, always
buckets, galvanized and shining.

What is this? Michael asks,
and I can't answer. There's no custom
I've ever witnessed that sends hundreds
of Hispanics in procession in this way.

And so I roll down the Datsun's window
and call out, *Qué es eso?* to the first man
we see returning on the left. *Tequila!*
he shouts and raises two buckets,
full to sloshing over, the liquor
pouring down his wrists and hands.

Then two miles up the road all lined
with walkers, we see the tank truck
on its side in the ravine, the people
with their buckets, filling up.

Last Night in Mexico, 1973

Even this close to midnight,
it's one hundred and five
at the southern edge of the desert.
Out of gas with no place open,
we put our money down in La Heredia,
the last hotel in Los Mochis.
After an eight-hour drive from Mazatlan,
the Datsun's coated with saffron dust,
half-moons like lizards' eyes
cut into the windshield.
Tomorrow before dawn,
we'll head for the border at Nogales,
but now we rise along iron banisters
up the hotel's central staircase
through four full floors of heat.
On each landing is a water cooler,
its aqua bubble drained dry for hours,
white paper cones like dunce-caps
scattered on the floor.
The building has no fans or air conditioners,
and our room is not deluxe,
so we have no windows either.
It's way too hot to even bitch
so when it's time to try for sleep,
we settle in to face the sweat,
the flicker of gnats,
and two clear scorching truths:
Sometimes you've got to do without.
Sometimes a bed is just a place
to lie in wait for morning.

Driving Away

(for Michael Hast, a true traveler at heart, 1949-1978)

Michael,
the day you went back
to the Cumberland earth,
the rest of us drove
in stone silence
down to Baltimore.
Some two hours after
we left your mother's home,
on a bluff above the highway,
a stallion stood,
blazing white
against blue and summer green.
Above his head,
a raven circled,
pinfeathers rising like breath
in the June heat.
The black bird hovered
and the horse stood still
as our Pontiac did seventy
back to the city.
Did others see this?
I don't know,
but I do
to this day—
while writing here,
in staring moments,
each time I drive away again
from the falling sun
and Blue Ridge Mountains
on this road
you left behind.

The Night War Ended

(August 9, 1974)

His skull whiter than death,
a mime worked the crowd
in the street cafe
where we'd gone that night
to drink in San Francisco.
He watched as we all did
on the flickering screen
above the bar
dark silhouettes of
helicopters lifting people off
the embassy roof
a world and many months away.
We watched choppers being
pushed into the sea
and Chicago and Washington
boiling with protest,
the searing effects of tear gas
as war came
into our living rooms,
Americans tearing at each other
through the Watergate
that moonless night
when a President,
himself deathly white,
announced his resignation.
Around us people lifted
glasses of dry red wine.
They clapped and cheered.
The mime began to dance.
We headed home,
made love till dawn,
giving peace a chance.

Missed Photo, Glacier Park

(Montana, 1974)

When we realized it was a grizzly
behind that boulder,
a nine-footer maybe,
on his hind legs, arching
his neck and sniffing the wind,
we retreated down the trail
and waited an hour or so.

Deciding not to change our
route and hike an extra day,
talking loudly and banging
pots together, we passed
that rock again and rounded
the curve where a deer carcass
lay ripped across the trail.

Two hundred yards above
a torrent of snow melt,
below and behind us, the bear
tore down the rubble field
and through the river
that would have washed
any man away.

When he bounded out
on the other side
and shook himself,
his blond-tipped coat
flashing in the sun,
unable to focus,
I dropped my camera.

It's taken me
over forty years
and this poem
to understand that
that was one picture
I would never need
to take.

First Anniversary

(Trident Villas, Jamaica, 1976)

Yeah, this was my idea
of a first anniversary,
flying to Montego, then driving
the length of Jamaica to Port Antonio,
and everything might have gone well
except for that flu bug that bit Jane
mid-flight, transforming
what I had envisioned
as a seven-hour ride through Paradise
into a journey through Hell.

I should have suspected trouble
when I bucked the rented Renault
out of the barbed wire parking lot,
praying as I climbed behind the wheel
that this learning to drive
shifting on the left
and steering on the right
wouldn't turn into what
the grinning guy behind the counter called
a crash course.

The first hour was postcard perfect
as we forged our way through cane fields
ten to twelve feet high,
driving onto vistas of beach and azure sea.
But then there was that wrong turn
where three guys with dreads and dusty eyes
waved us deeper into the woods,
and later, a town not on the map
where little kids lined the street shouting,
It's a white lady, it's a white lady.

And maybe I shouldn't mention us
careening around a mountain curve,
a school bus on our bumper
and Jane's head out the window
or that wait for forty minutes
in a pass through the Blue Mountains
as the wreckage was cleared
where a moped had struck a mule.
And nothing had prepared us
for the streets of Port Antonio.

On this Jamaican Independence Night,
thousands of celebrants jammed the boulevard,
swigging rum and setting off Roman candles.
The river of people parted as I hung
a hard right down a side street
and crawled out of the car to address
the only person in the town who didn't appear
to be dancing. Ninety-five and stooped over
with her straw grocery bag, this lady,
hobbling home from madness, directed us.

She up dot road, our savior said
in patois, pointing south to the Trident,
where ten minutes later,
we found ourselves
standing on oriental rugs
in a room with potted palms
as I registered
and Jane ran outside into the bushes
to celebrate
our anniversary again.

Question & Answer

(Jamaica, 1977)

What's that? Jane asked
while steering the Renault
around a crescent curve
near the cane plantations on the coast.
Just after dawn on New Year's Day,
we were heading from Port Antonio
through the Blue Mountains,
driving the length of the island
to catch our flight back home.

Silent, I was staring
into a field as dark as death
where a man, near naked,
hunched over a thin snake of smoke
rising from a fire beneath his hands.
As we sped by, he rocked back
on his heels to glare at us
through the eyes of a voodoo mask.
Keep going, I replied.

What the Fodor's Guide Didn't Tell Us

(Santa Marta, Colombia, 1979)

His Spanish was perfect
as behind mirrored glasses,
he requested his boarding pass
at the Avianca counter
at Miami International
with people I sensed were mostly
in the trade. He sat beside us
in the window seat and introduced
himself in perfect English as Tony,
an American on the way to Colombia
on oil business for his father
who lived in Louisiana and Venezuela
and sometimes in Colombia
where Tony stated he'd been raised
on an inland ranch.

And he didn't even blink
as minutes east of the fortress
on the coast of Cartagena,
the plane went down
for two unscheduled stops in the dark,
picking up passengers, mostly men
in T-shirts and jeans, without luggage,
including one bronze-haired black man
in boots and a white cowboy hat
who was brown-bagging tequila
as he was greeted by others on the plane
as Red.

When we landed in Santa Marta,
two hundred yards from the terminal,
soldiers with automatic weapons drawn
surrounded the plane and herded
all fifty of us passengers
to the customs lines
to have our luggage searched.
Without speaking, Tony pulled
an inch-thick wad of bills
from his sportcoat pocket
and handed it to a guard
who passed his briefcase, unopened,
through an iron gate to someone
waiting in the crowd.

Once through customs and on the curb,
Tony hailed a cab for us,
driven by a man he said we could trust
to deliver us to the beach hotel
where the next day we saw Red
cruising the Caribbean like a king
in a forty-foot Donzi
and where, after the airport closed,
we could hear planes taking off and landing
through the night.

On the Ground in Medellín

(Colombia, 1979)

As soon as the plane hit the ground in Medellín,
an announcement crackled over the intercom
and most of the passengers stood,
grabbed their luggage, and hustled off.
Our Spanish was much too slow
and their departure much too quick,
so, resigned to confusion,
Jane and I settled into our Avianca seats,
mine which wouldn't stay in the upright position,
hers with a seatbelt missing its buckle half.
Finally a businessman filled us in—
we could have saved several hours
of flight time to Cali
if we'd departed with the others.
Faded and air-worn, we watched
our former fellow passengers
across the tarmac climbing the stairs
into the waiting plane.
Below us, cargo doors slammed shut,
signaling the last of the leaving luggage.
Just as the bags arrived
at the other plane's side,
its passenger stairs were wheeled away
and the cargo men looked up in shock,
shouted, and began to scatter.
The jet's engines whistled,
then roared to life,
an orange blast propelling
what was left of the unloaded baggage
through the air for fifty yards,
suitcases blowing open, clothing sailing
open-armed into a chain-link fence.

Down the runway,
the plane lifted off to Cali
as two little men on bicycles
came out to gather what was left.
In our plane, Jane and I looked at each other,
smiled a little, and thanked God
our language skills were poor.

A Prayer of Thanksgiving

I have camped near streams in Wyoming where the brown trout were thick enough to walk on.

I've hiked the Tetons on the fourth of July in snow up to my waist and slept in the Jersey Pine Barrens in January when men in canoes and headlamps came up the rivers in the darkest hour of night, my canteen water freezing between quick sips by the fire.

I've turned blue with the best of them in a rock-dammed pool in the Andes and a rock-slide lake above Ireland's Conor Pass.

Perched by a lake in Colorado at 11,000 feet, I have watched the sun explode into orange behind the black ridge of the Rockies then climbed to a mountain peak the next day at 13,000, my brain flashing red for oxygen.

I've swum in a pool in Yosemite so deep and clear that I could see my fear at the bottom and lain awake beside it that night beneath the falling stars.

I've slid down snow chutes on Rainier on 80-degree days in August, made love with the mountain over my left and right shoulders.

I've witnessed the smelt run on the North Pacific shores, deer striding onto the beach at Big Sur, moose up to their antlers in a pond south of Katahdin.

In Mexico, I've waited out the mist to photograph volcanoes, raised both hands to the sky atop the Pyramid of the Sun.

And now, years later, I realize what this means.

I have done these things, I have done these things, I have done these things.

Amen.

IV

Dreams

"...it is only after seeing man
as his unconscious,
revealed by his dreams,
presents him to us
that we shall understand him fully."

—Sigmund Freud,
The Interpretation of Dreams

Dream Poem: Babes at Sea

No land in sight,
the sea's as flat as a countertop,
and I'm in the middle of it,
treading water to beat the band.
Over the side of a shallow dinghy,
a woman's hands lift infants,
setting them afloat
in Mickey Mouse kiddie tubes,
open at the back.
One after another they're set in—
ten, eleven, twelve.
Some cry, barely able
to keep their heads up.
Others coo, bobbing
like ducks in a carnival booth.
My job, of course, is to protect them,
save them if they slide or tip,
so I'm hustling, hustling,
though I'm just a kid myself.
Another child's coming over the side
when I see it, a white wall,
a water spout, huge and rumbling,
bearing down on the boat.
Half-panicked but still in charge,
I hand them back, child after child,
into the woman's hands, lifting,
scooping babies to safety,
but when I turn to grab the last one,
he's gone,
a ripple on the mirror surface,
and all at once,
I know that child
is me.

Dream Poem: Deep City

My sister, brother and I
walk wide-eyed
along an asphalt river,
following a sound
whose source we cannot see.
A neon sky muffles the moon.
Around us, tier after tier of
rowhouses rise like curses
to angry Mayan gods.
The canyon walls are cool concrete,
riveted with windows.

Kathy, six and curly-haired,
clings to my side,
both arms flung
around my chest,
while Tom childsteps,
trying to keep my hand.
Flecked with glass and bits of shell,
the asphalt glides like fever.
On either side, fountains
of grey burst from the earth,
splashing into steam.

I, the middle child,
am the first to make out voices.
They float like summer thunder,
distant, rolling, barely heard,
as we strain to understand.
Then the voices grow distinct,
not words we know,
but songs of blood and breathing.

Like threats, they loom,
grow larger, louder,
cascading from the walls.

Finally, we see them,
the source of sound.
Shadow men,
with day-glo eyes
and stiletto teeth,
they crowd each window,
leap between balconies
above us, waving,
chanting, leering down,
enticing us to wander in
to die in the deep,

deep city.

The Planting, 1980

Back when I was certain
that beauty was order
and order meant control,
I'd spend full days
in the garden, turning soil,
turning away from trouble.
One April morning, I put in azaleas,
scarlet globes spaced evenly
against the chain-link fence.
The holes were perfect circles,
six inches larger than
the tightly burlapped roots.
I tamped the soil, fertilized,
and bedded down the plants
in still-steaming hardwood mulch.

That night, tumbling into
the chaos I called sleep,
I walked the yard again,
but the plants were gone,
and in their circles,
the soil was bubbling,
seething with boiling blood.
In each space lay men
dismembered—
the fool I worked for,
the body of a teacher,
hole after hole filled with
folks I wanted gone.

One year later, the azaleas
were withered, yellowed,
dropping leaves,
victims of the shade.
I took them out,
gave them to a neighbor.
In their place,
I put in sneezeweed,
dug up by the highway,
scattered by birds and wind.
Until I moved,
those stray plants flourished,
a riot of yellow taking over
the yard. In my mind,
they owned the place. The time
for my planting was over.

The Cause Unknown

(Dreams/Newsflashes, July 11-13, 1991)

In the dream,
the river is a hundred yards wide,
the banks lush with skunk cabbage and jack-in-the-pulpit.

A six-year-old Baltimore girl died tonight,
caught in a crossfire of semi-automatics.
She was struck in the head while sitting on a curb on Rosedale
Street.

The river slides by slowly,
its water thick as syrup,
cool as your grandmother's hands.
Its surface is dusted with yellow pollen.

Police officials say the girl's murder
was part of a drug turf war.
A twenty-year-old Anne Arundel County man
has surrendered himself in the case.

I'm on the near shore,
heading down to the river's edge.
The air is the color of emeralds.
In my hand I have a shepherd's crook,
worn hickory, polished from years of use.

In Overlea today, a pair of men abducted
a woman and her two daughters.
They forced the woman to drive
to Sequoia Federal Savings Bank, where she worked,
to empty a cash drawer for them.

The river bank is spongy;
water sloshes around my shoes.
I sense the earth beneath me floating, raft-like,
and I'm hard-pressed to keep my balance.

The men vandalized the woman's home
and raped her eldest daughter.
Two suspects are being held in the case.
Both men have prior criminal records.

I begin to probe the weeds along the river's edge,
using my staff to pull back the bloom of algae.
I see a flash of white, then the full, cold hand of a man.
His face floats up, wax gray and blue;
his eyes stare, wide open.

A fifty-nine-year-old bank teller in West Baltimore
was fatally wounded today as she sat in her van,
waiting for the bank to open. The assailants accosted
the woman in the parking lot of the Maryland National Bank
on West Franklintown Road where she worked.

Another body appears, a woman,
hair flaring like Medusa's, eyes gazing at the sky.
Still pulling back the shore, I see more hands, faces, eyes.
I'm treading on bodies, barely able to stand.

Police say the woman was shot twice with a high caliber handgun,
the assailants reportedly fleeing in a Mazda. One suspect
in the case appeared to be suffering from a gunshot wound.
Police are searching for him in hospital emergency rooms.

On the other side of the river, I see Jane and the children,
happy, joking, ready for a picnic. Laughing, Jane calls to me
for directions, looking for a place for the children and her to cross.

At 6:30 this morning a man staggered into The Right Place Bar
in Baltimore, a victim of a homicide attempt.
The man had been shot in the nose and was bleeding from his
mouth.

Keep them away, I scream to Jane, keep them away,
but she doesn't seem to hear me. Below me the earth begins to slide,
revealing hundreds of cadavers. Unable to stand the sight, I shut my eyes.

While the bar owner dialed 911, the wounded man
looked out the door and saw his assailants, five men,
coming down Pratt Street after him.

Keep them away, I scream. Keep them away.

In the Inner Harbor today, police recovered the body
of a forty-four-year-old blind man from Towson. The man's
identity is being withheld pending notification of next of kin.

The cause of the apparent drowning is unknown.

The cause of the apparent drowning is unknown.

The Night of the Dream

(April 27, 2011)

In the dream, I'm driving
north to upstate New York,
feeling lost,
the sky silver,
the weather odd,
and I need to see Ray,
my college roommate
from forty years ago.
Then I'm in a dorm room
in a chrome-fronted building
I don't recognize.
The door opens,
and Ray walks in.
I'm glad you're here, I tell him.
I'm glad you're here,
hugging him,
clapping him on the back.

Three nights later I get
a voice mail from Ray
from Alabama, a crackly tape
that sounds like he's talking
through a storm.
I'm OK, he says, *the house
is OK, but the power's out,
probably for a week.
My phone's going;
I'll be in touch.*

The next night I call him,
and he picks up to tell the story
of tornados ripping through Huntsville,
one funnel cloud moving
right down his street
then veering off,
other houses being cut to pieces
by falling trees.
The night of the dream,
he had been huddling
in his bathroom
in the dark
with water and blankets
and a radio, hoping
the batteries would hold out.
I'm glad you're here, I tell him.
I'm glad you're here.

Dream Poems:
Before the Decision to Retire

I.

I'm on a granite mountaintop,
like one on the coast of Maine,
longing to go down to the beach
which I can see a mile below.
Jane, retired, is waiting there,
and the water is deep blue.
The path down, sun-lit, wanders
through hemlocks and pines.
You'll need this, two men,
the gatekeepers, tell me,
as they hold out a ticket,
white, as flimsy as a receipt.
As I reach for it, it's taken
by a gust of wind.
Scrambling, I chase it over boulders,
but before I can catch it,
it blows over the edge of a cliff
and disappears.

I do this because I love kids. They make it all worthwhile.
—one of my teaching mantras

In a canyon of concrete,
I'm drawn to the edge
of a roaring waterfall
that drops thirty feet
into a bottomless pool.
In the water, a policeman
floats face down,
the victim of a monster
I sense but cannot see.
Then huge hands grab my shoulders
and try to push me over the edge as well.
The cement is slick and shiny
so I can't resist the sliding,
the monster gripping me
as I struggle.
Behind us, I feel somebody watching,
and I twist around to see a group
of ten or fifteen children,
maybe eight years old, staring,
fascinated.
Help me, please, help me,
I scream to them.
In silence, they stand
and watch.

Dream Poem:
The Tightrope Walkers

The rope I'm looking down curves
like a bridge span into the horizon,
and I'm treading it, barely balanced,
as the middle man of three tightrope
walkers heading to some brilliance
in the distance. We're 20,000 feet
into the air, sometimes above the clouds,
looking down on the green farmland
of my childhood in Frederick County.
I keep my balance, placing my hands
on the lead man's shoulders,
the man behind me holding me by the waist
to prevent my slipping.
We're moving quickly,
walking with purpose, mile by mile
along this rope as thick as my arm.
As the rope slopes up, I see our destination,
a door blazing like the sun.
As we reach it, I look back into the distance.
What about them? I ask.
They'll be fine, the other walkers tell me
as we pass through the door
and spread our wings
to fly.

Acknowledgments

I'd like to thank Gary Blankenburg, a fine poet and teacher and a great friend, for his support and encouragement throughout my writing career. I especially thank him for his invaluable advice and assistance in editing this book.

I'd also like to thank Sara Jones Cleary, a fine writer and editor and a wonderful daughter, for her assistance in proofing and preparing my manuscript for publication.

Finally, thanks to the editors of the following publications in which the listed poems first appeared, some in slightly different form:

The Baltimore Sun: "A Teacher's Thoughts at Graduation"
The City Paper: "Terrapin"
The Connecticut River Review: "Thought, While Walking with My Two-Year-Old Daughter"
Dancing Shadow Review: "Going Back to Bill's," "Walking with Nathan"
Dream International Quarterly: "Dream Poem: Deep City," "The Planting, 1980"
Free State Review: "Dream Poems: Before the Decision to Retire"
Gargoyle: "On the Ground in Medellín," "What the Fodor's Guide Didn't Tell Us," "What I Know About Anthrax"
Harford Poetry Review: "Even When You Think It's Winter"
Little Patuxent Review: "Physics for Poets"
Loch Raven Review: "Debridement," "Learning to Walk, Baltimore, 1973," "The Night of the Dream," "The Night War Ended," "Three Times Seeing Quentin"
The Lyric: "House Sounds, 1 A.M."
Maryland Poetry Review: "Dream Poem: Babes at Sea," "Dream Poem: The Tightrope Walkers"
Passager: "Three Men in the Hospital, Shaving"
The Pearl: "Nightsong, 3 A.M."
Studio One: "College Boy"
Swimming at Night (chapbook, winner of the 1992 Baltimore ARTSCAPE Literary Arts Award for Poetry): "Catching Fireflies," "The Cause Unknown,""Chain, Lake Goshen, VA, 1963" "Dawn, A Monday Morning," "Driving Away," "Lesson: Looking at the Moon," "Morning Poem, Dividing Creek, 1957," "Mother Country, 2 A.M." *Plane Crashes in Towson, Killing Pilot*," "Sanctuary"

About the Author

Bill Jones, a longtime writer and teacher, lives with his wife, Jane Croghan Jones, in Baltimore, Maryland. His poetry has appeared in *The Baltimore Review, Borderlands: The Texas Poetry Review, California Quarterly, The Comstock Review, The Connecticut River Review, Gargoyle, Loch Raven Review, Passager,* and numerous other publications. He is a past recipient of a Baltimore Artscape Literary Arts Award for Poetry for his chapbook *Swimming at Night.*

Apprentice House is the country's only campus-based, student-staffed book publishing company. Directed by professors and industry professionals, it is a nonprofit activity of the Communication Department at Loyola University Maryland.

Using state-of-the-art technology and an experiential learning model of education, Apprentice House publishes books in untraditional ways. This dual responsibility as publishers and educators creates an unprecedented collaborative environment among faculty and students, while teaching tomorrow's editors, designers, and marketers.

Outside of class, progress on book projects is carried forth by the AH Book Publishing Club, a co-curricular campus organization supported by Loyola University Maryland's Office of Student Activities.

Eclectic and provocative, Apprentice House titles intend to entertain as well as spark dialogue on a variety of topics. Financial contributions to sustain the press's work are welcomed. Contributions are tax deductible to the fullest extent allowed by the IRS.

To learn more about Apprentice House books or to obtain submission guidelines, please visit www.apprenticehouse.com.

Apprentice House
Communication Department
Loyola University Maryland
4501 N. Charles Street
Baltimore, MD 21210
Ph: 410-617-5265 • Fax: 410-617-2198
info@apprenticehouse.com • www.apprenticehouse.com